M000102072

LANGUAGE ARTS
INSTANT ASSESSMENTS
for Data Tracking
Grade 2

Credits
Author: Hope Spencer

Visit *carsondellosa.com* for correlations to Common Core, state, national, and Canadian provincial standards.

Carson-Dellosa Publishing, LLC
PO Box 35665
Greensboro, NC 27425 USA
carsondellosa.com

978-1-4838-3617-1
01-339161151

✦ Table of Contents ✦

Assessment and Data Tracking............. 3
Types of Assessment 4
How to Use This Book........................ 5
Exit Tickets 7

Reading: Literature
Show What You Know........................ 9
Before, During, and After
    Reading Prompts....................... 11
Understanding Key Details 17
Making Inferences 18
Character Analysis 19
Character Descriptions.................... 20
Retelling Fables............................. 21
Details in Poetry 22
Exit Tickets 23

Reading: Informational Text
Show What You Know...................... 25
Before, During, and After
    Reading Prompts....................... 27
Main Idea 33
Determining the Meanings of Words... 34
Making the Connection
    between Ideas 35
Sequencing Steps........................... 36
Cause and Effect............................ 37
Using Text Features......................... 38
Exit Tickets 39

Reading: Foundational Skills
Show What You Know...................... 41
Word Lists: Decoding Words 43
Fluency Passages 45
Fluency Passages:
    Comprehension Questions 53
Exit Tickets 54

Writing
Writing Prompts............................. 55
Editing for Grammar, Spelling, and
    Capitalization.......................... 59
Revising Writing 60
Exit Tickets 61

Language
Show What You Know: Conventions .. 63
Show What You Know: Language...... 67
Word Lists: Parts of Speech 69
Word Lists: Vocabulary 70
Plural Nouns................................. 71
Collective Nouns............................ 72
Irregular Plural Nouns..................... 73
Reflexive Pronouns......................... 74
Identifying Verbs 75
Past Tense Verbs............................ 76
Adjectives and Adverbs 77
Identifying Parts of Speech 78
Compound Sentences 79
Capitalization............................... 80
Commas in Letters 81
Contractions................................. 82
Possessive Nouns 83
Prefixes and Suffixes....................... 84
Compound Words........................... 85
Context Clues 86
Exit Tickets 87

Answer Key................................... 91

✦ Assessment and Data Tracking ✦

Data tracking is an essential element in modern classrooms. Teachers are often required to capture student learning through both formative and summative assessments. They then must use the results to guide teaching, remediation, and lesson planning and provide feedback to students, parents, and administrators. Because time is always at a premium in the classroom, it is vital that teachers have the assessments they need at their fingertips. The assessments need to be suited to the skill being assessed as well as adapted to the stage in the learning process. This is true for an informal checkup at the end of a lesson or a formal assessment at the end of a unit.

This book will provide the tools and assessments needed to determine your students' level of mastery throughout the school year. The assessments are both formal and informal and include a variety of formats—pretests and posttests, flash cards, prompt cards, traditional tests, and exit tickets. Often, there are several assessment options for a single skill or concept to allow you the greatest flexibility when assessing understanding. Simply select the assessment that best fits your needs, or use them all to create a comprehensive set of assessments for before, during, and after learning.

Incorporate Instant Assessments into your daily plans to streamline the data-tracking process and keep the focus on student mastery and growth.

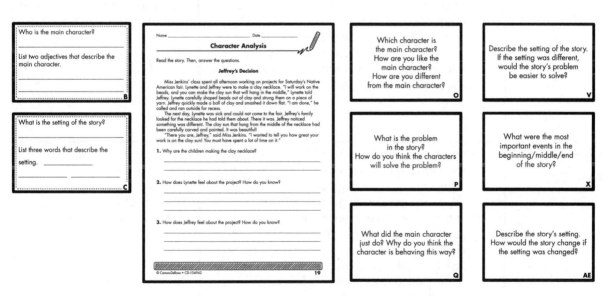

A variety of instant assessments for story elements

Types of Assessment

Assessment usually has a negative association because it brings to mind tedious pencil-and-paper tests and grading. However, it can take on many different forms and be a positive, integral part of the year. Not all assessments need to be formal, nor do they all need to be graded. Choose the type of assessment to use based on the information you need to gather. Then, you can decide if or how it should be graded.

	What Does It Look Like?	Examples
Formative Assessment	• occurs during learning • is administered frequently • is usually informal and not graded • identifies areas of improvement • provides immediate feedback so a student can make adjustments promptly, if needed • allows teachers to rethink strategies, lesson content, etc., based on current student performance • is process-focused • has the most impact on a student's performance	• in-class observations • exit tickets • reflections and journaling • homework • student-teacher conferences • student self-evaluations
Interim Assessment	• occurs occasionally • is more formal and usually graded • feedback is not immediate, though still fairly quick • helps teachers identify gaps in teaching and areas for remediation • often includes performance assessments, which are individualized, authentic, and performance-based in order to evaluate higher-level thinking skills	• in-class observations • exit tickets • reflections and journaling • homework • student-teacher conferences • student self-evaluations
Summative Assessment	• occurs once learning is considered complete • the information is used by the teacher and school for broader purposes • takes time to return a grade or score • can be used to compare a student's performance to others • is product-focused • has the least impact on a student's performance since there are few or no opportunities for retesting	• cumulative projects • final portfolios • quarterly testing • end-of-the-year testing • standardized testing

The assessments in this book follow a few different formats, depending on the skill or concept being assessed. Use the descriptions below to familiarize yourself with each unique format and get the most out of Instant Assessments all year long.

Show What You Know

Most anchors begin with two *Show What You Know* tests. They follow the same format with the same types of questions, so they can be used as a pretest and posttest that can be directly compared to show growth. Or, use one as a test at the end of a unit and use the second version as a retest for students after remediation.

Exit Tickets

Most anchors end with exit tickets that cover the variety of concepts within the anchor. Exit tickets are very targeted questions designed to assess understanding of specific skills, so they are ideal formative assessments to use at the end of a lesson. Exit tickets do not have space for student names, allowing teachers to gather information on the entire class without placing pressure on individual students. If desired, have students write their names or initials on the back of the tickets. Other uses for exit tickets include the following:

- Use the back of each ticket for longer answers, fuller explanations, or extension questions. If needed, students can staple them to larger sheets of paper.
- They can also be used for warm-ups or to find out what students know before a lesson.
- Use the generic exit tickets on pages 7 and 8 for any concept you want to assess. Be sure to fill in any blanks before copying.
- Laminate them and place them in a language arts center as task cards.
- Use them to play Scoot or a similar review game at the end of a unit.
- Choose several to create a targeted assessment for a skill or set of skills.

Word Lists

Word lists consist of several collections of grade-appropriate words in areas that students need to be assessed in, such as sight words, spelling patterns, and words with affixes. They are not comprehensive but are intended to make creating your own assessments simpler. Use the word lists to create vocabulary tests, word decoding fluency tests, spelling lists, etc., for the year.

Cards

Use the cards as prompts for one-on-one conferencing. Simply copy the cards, cut them apart, and follow the directions preceding each set of cards. Use the lettering to keep track of which cards a student has interacted with.

- Copy on card stock and/or laminate for durability.
- Punch holes in the top left corners and place the cards on a book ring to make them easily accessible.
- Copy the sets on different colors of paper to keep them easily separated or to distinguish different sections within a set of cards.
- Easily differentiate by using different amounts or levels of cards to assess a student.
- Write the answers on the backs of cards to create self-checking flash cards.
- Place them in a language arts center as task cards or matching activities.
- Use them to play Scoot or a similar review game at the end of a unit.

Assessment Pages

The reproducible assessment pages are intended for use as a standard test of a skill. Use them in conjunction with other types of assessment to get a full picture of a student's level of understanding. They can also be used for review or homework.

Fluency Pages

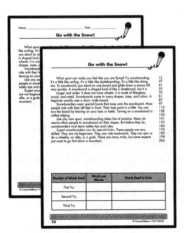

Use the paired fluency pages to assess students' oral reading fluency. Provide a copy of the student page to the student, and use the teacher copy to track how far the student read, which words he or she struggled with, and the student's performance on repeated readings. The word count is provided at the end of each line for easy totaling. Then, use the related comprehension questions to assess the student's understanding of what he or she read.

Exit Tickets

Exit tickets are a useful formative assessment tool that you can easily work into your day. You can choose to use a single exit ticket at the end of the day or at the end of each lesson. Simply choose a ticket below and make one copy for each student. Then, have students complete the prompt and present them to you as their ticket out of the door. Use the student responses to gauge overall learning, create small remediation groups, or target areas for reteaching. A blank exit ticket is included on page 8 so you can create your own exit tickets as well.

What stuck with you today?

_____
_____
_____
_____

List three facts you learned today. Put them in order from most important to least important.

1. _____
2. _____
3. _____

The first thing I'll tell my family about today is

_____
_____
_____
_____.

The most important thing I learned today is

_____
_____
_____
_____.

Color the face that shows how you feel about understanding today's lesson.

Explain why. _____
_____

Summarize today's lesson in 10 words or less.

_____
_____
_____
_____

One example of _____

is _____

_____

_____

_____ .

One question I still have is _____

_____

_____

_____

_____ .

How will understanding _____

_____

help you in real life? _____

_____

_____

One new word I learned today is

_____ .

It means _____

_____

_____ .

Draw a picture related to the lesson.
Add a caption.

_____

_____

If today's lesson were a song, the title

would be _____

_____

because _____

_____ .

The answer is _____ .

What is the question? _____

_____

_____

_____

Name _____ Date _____

✦ Show What You Know ✦
Reading: Literature

Read the story. Then, answer the questions.

Grandpa's New Job

My grandpa was a firefighter for a long time. He helped save people from burning houses. Sometimes, he carried people down a ladder. Now, he has a new job. He does not go into burning buildings anymore. Grandpa visits schools to share **knowledge** about fire safety. He shows students the burn marks on his old coat. He tells everyone how to stay safe. My grandpa is a hero.

1. Who was a firefighter?

_____

2. Who is the main character of the story?

_____

3. What is the meaning of the word **knowledge**?

_____

_____

4. Write three adjectives that could describe the word *fire*.

_____   _____   _____

5. List three things that Grandpa does in his new job.

_____   _____

_____

6. How does the author feel about Grandpa? How do you know?

_____

_____

Name _____ Date _____

Read the story. Then, answer the questions.

A Really Great Gardener

Grace Chang could make anything grow. If she planted an apple seed, an apple tree would grow by morning. The apples would peel themselves and hop into the nearest pie crust. If she planted cottonseeds, sweaters would spring up overnight. One day, Grace planted a kernel of corn. It grew and grew. People came from all over the state to see it. It grew so big that Grace opened a café inside of it. She served the best corn bread in the state!

1. Who is the main character of the story? _____

2. List three things that Grace plants.

   _____   _____   _____

3. Grace is the same as other gardeners in some ways. What does she do that is the same as other gardeners?

   _____

   _____

4. Grace is different from other gardeners in some way. What happens that makes her different from other gardeners?

   _____

   _____

5. How do you know this story is a tall tale?

   _____

   _____

   _____

Before, During, and After
Reading Prompts

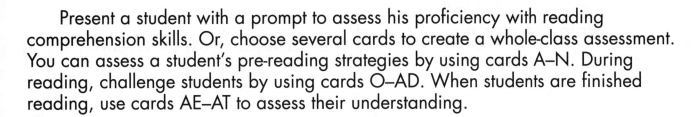

Present a student with a prompt to assess his proficiency with reading comprehension skills. Or, choose several cards to create a whole-class assessment. You can assess a student's pre-reading strategies by using cards A–N. During reading, challenge students by using cards O–AD. When students are finished reading, use cards AE–AT to assess their understanding.

Read the title. What do you think the story will be about?

A

What do you think the topic of the story will be? Write two things you already know about the topic.

B

Look at the picture. What does the picture tell you about the story?

C

Read the first sentence. What does the first sentence tell you about the story?

D

Scan the story. Find two or more words that you do not know. Write each word and determine its meaning. What do the meanings of these words tell you about the story?

E

Do you think there will be a problem in the story? Why or why not?

F

Why did the author
write the story?

G

Choose three words from
the story. Use the words
in sentences as you
predict what the story
will be about.

H

Do you think the story will take
place in the past, the present,
or the future? What clues
are you using to make your
prediction?

I

Scan the story and look for
repeated words. Use the
words to write questions you
have about the story.

J

Scan the story. Do you see
anything that reminds you of
another story you have read?
Explain your answer.

K

Look at the title and any
illustrations. Do you think the
story is real or make-believe?
Explain your answer.

L

Find words that are repeated
in the story. What do these
words tell you about the story?

M

Why do you want to
read this story?

N

Which character is
the main character?
How are you like the
main character?
How are you different?

O

What is the problem
in the story?
How do you think the characters
will solve the problem?

P

What did the main character
just do? Why do you think the
character is behaving this way?

Q

How have your feelings about
the main character changed
since the beginning of the story?

R

Is any part of the story
confusing to you? Explain.

S

List three adjectives to describe
the main character. Would you
use these three adjectives to
describe anyone you know?

T

What does the main character
most need or want?

U

Describe the setting of the story.
If the setting was different,
would the story's problem
be easier to solve? Explain.

V

Describe one picture from the story. Explain how it helped you understand the story.

W

What were the most important events in the beginning/middle/end of the story?

X

What questions do you have about the story so far?

Y

What does this story remind you of?

Z

Choose one character trait the main character has that you would like to have. Explain your choice.

AA

Check your fluency. Are you reading too fast or too slow? Are you pausing at periods and other punctuation marks?

AB

Retell the events of the story so far. If you could write the rest of the story, what would you write?

AC

Pretend that you are one of the characters in the story. Explain an event in the story from your point of view.

AD

Describe the story's setting. How would the story change if the setting was changed?

AE

Read another story. Tell three ways the two stories are similar. Tell three ways the two stories are different.

AF

Is the author trying to teach a lesson? What lesson is he or she trying to teach?

AG

Which character would you most want to be friends with? Why?

AH

If you could change one thing about the story, what would you change? Why?

AI

Do you like the way the story ended? Why or why not?

AJ

Did the author write this story to persuade, to inform, or to entertain? How do you know?

AK

When the story's problem was solved, did it cause another problem?

AL

Compare the main character
in this story to the main
character in another story.
How are they alike?
How are they different?

AM

Does this story remind you of
another story? Explain.

AN

How do the characters feel
at the beginning of the story?
How do they feel at
the end of the story?

AO

What was the most exciting
part of the story?

AP

If you could ask the author a
question about the story,
what would you ask?

AQ

Give a short summary
of the story.

AR

Describe the problem in
the story. What could the
characters have done
to avoid the problem?

AS

Which parts of the story
could really happen?
Which parts of the story
could not really happen?

AT

Name _____ Date _____

Understanding Key Details

Read the story. Then, answer the questions.

A Sweet Clue

Mrs. Flores asked her students if they had seen her favorite blue pen with stars on it. Joseph looked at Kyle and whispered, "It sounds like a mystery."

At recess break, Joseph talked to Mrs. Flores. "May we look at the crime scene?" There was a brown spot on the clean desk.

Kyle asked Mrs. Flores if she had eaten any chocolate that day. "No," sighed Mrs. Flores, "but I wish I had some now."

Joseph looked in the trash can. The boys looked at all of the students' faces as they walked in the door.

After school, the boys went to see Mr. Burke. Mr. Burke loved chocolate. Kyle and Joseph saw Mr. Burke in the hallway. He had a blue pen in his pocket.

"Is that your pen, Mr. Burke?" asked Joseph.

"Well, no," he said as he patted his pocket. "I borrowed it from someone."

"Did you find it on Mrs. Flores's desk?" asked Kyle.

"Yes, I did. I guess I better give it back to her."

"Case closed," said the boys.

1. Mrs. Flores has a problem. What is it? _____

_____

2. What clue do the boys find? _____

_____

3. Why hasn't Mr. Burke returned the pen? _____

_____

4. How do you think the boys feel after they talk to Mr. Burke? _____

_____

_____

Making Inferences

Read the story. Then, answer the questions.

A Cookie Contest

Dan's hands shook as he worked. This was a big deal. These cookies were special. David had practiced the recipe for weeks. It was finally time. He was at the Cookie Baking Championship!

Dan measured the sugar. He stirred the dough with care. Then, he looked around. It was time to add his secret ingredient. He did not want anyone to see. Dan quickly scooped out some oats. He dropped them into the bowl before anyone saw him. Then, he rolled the dough into balls. He put the balls on the baking sheet and slid it into the oven.

The judges tasted each cookie. The three of them met in the corner to talk. When they finished, they gave Dan the blue ribbon! Dan was so happy! One judge stopped him.

"May I please have your recipe?" she asked. "I can't tell what is in your cookies."

1. Write the numbers 1–4 to put the events in order.

_____ Dan scooped out some oats.   _____ Dan measured the sugar.

_____ Dan put the baking sheet into the oven.   _____ Dan rolled the dough into balls.

2. How does Dan feel about the contest?
   A. He does not care about it.
   B. He is nervous and excited.
   C. He wants to hide it.

3. Has Dan made these cookies before?
   A. This is the first time he has made the cookies.
   B. He has made them many times.
   C. He has watched his mother make the cookies before.

4. Do you think the oats helped Dan's cookies win the contest? _____

   Why or why not? _____

Character Analysis

Read the story. Then, answer the questions.

Jeffrey's Decision

Miss Jenkins's class spent all afternoon working on projects for Saturday's Native American Fair. Lynette and Jeffrey were to make a clay necklace. "I will work on the beads, and you can make the clay sun that will hang in the middle," Lynette told Jeffrey. Lynette carefully shaped beads out of clay and strung them on a piece of yarn. Jeffrey quickly made a ball of clay and smashed it down flat. "I am done," he called, and ran outside for recess.

The next day, Lynette was sick and could not come to the fair. Jeffrey's family looked for the necklace he had told them about. There it was. Jeffrey noticed something was different. The clay sun that hung from the middle of the necklace had been carefully carved and painted. It was beautiful!

"There you are, Jeffrey," said Miss Jenkins. "I wanted to tell you how great your work was on the clay sun! You must have spent a lot of time on it."

1. Why are the children making the clay necklace?

_____

_____

2. How does Lynette feel about the project? How do you know?

_____

_____

_____

3. How does Jeffrey feel about the project? How do you know?

_____

_____

_____

Name _____ Date _____

Character Descriptions

Read the story. Then, answer the questions.

Making a Friend

Ron is a new student. His classmates want to get to know him. They try to talk to him. Ron calls them names. He hides the ball at recess. The children are scared of him. They do not want to get to know him anymore.

One day, Ron is late to school. That morning, the teacher says, "Pretend you are the new student. You come to a new school where everyone knows each other. I think Ron was scared and he acted the way he did because he was scared."

Ron's classmates want to be his friend. They ask him to sit with them at lunch. They let him use the swings first during recess. They give him the newest paints in art class. Soon, Ron is very kind to the others. He takes turns at recess. He never says anything mean to anyone. His classmates learned an important lesson. Ron learned an important lesson too.

1. Write three adjectives that describe Ron at the beginning of the story.

_____   _____   _____

2. Write three adjectives that describe Ron at the end of the story.

_____   _____   _____

3. What lesson do you think Ron's classmates learned?

_____

_____

4. What lesson do you think Ron learned?

_____

_____

5. What do you think the class will do the next time there is a new student?

_____

_____

Retelling Fables

Read the story. Then, answer the questions.

Why Dogs' Ears Hang Down

Long ago, the animals wanted to plan a surprise party for the king. The dog was the king's best friend. The other animals did not think the dog could keep the secret. So, when they talked about the party, they folded down the dog's ears. This way, the dog could not hear the plans. "It's a surprise," they told the dog. The party was a big success. The dog loved being surprised. To this day, many dogs keep their ears down. They are hoping someone is planning a surprise party for them.

1. Why don't the animals want to tell the dog about the party plans?

    A. The party is for the dog.

    B. They do not think the dog can keep a secret.

    C. The king told them not to.

2. Why do dogs keep their ears down now?

    A. They are the king's best friends.

    B. They do not want to hear any secrets.

    C. They hope someone is planning a surprise party for them.

3. Write **T** for true and **F** for false.

_____ The animals told the dog about the party.

_____ The dog loved the surprise.

_____ The animals folded the dog's ears down.

_____ The dog wanted to have a party for the king.

4. What do you think would have happened if the animals had not folded the dog's ears down?

_____

_____

Details in Poetry

Read the poem. Then, answer the questions.

Look Out!

One very hot day, Ella Elephant said, "I think I may sneeze."
    So, the grassland animals said, "Excuse us, if you please."
And ran, they did, for they were afraid
    Of what would happen when Ella's sneeze was made.
The giraffes ran for cover. They hid behind leaves
    Of the thickest and tallest of all of the trees.
The warthogs got up from feeding on their knees.
    They frightfully asked, "Did Ella say she may sneeze?"
The falcon flew quickly as falcons can do.
    He remembered the last time Ella said, "Achoo!"
The earth had rumbled, and all the trees shook
    Worse than any disaster you've seen in a book.
So, the animals covered their ears. They closed their eyes.
    But then, they got a pleasant surprise . . .
Ella the Elephant did not let out a sneeze,
    Instead she laughed and made a slight breeze.
Now, all of the animals went back to their day.
    They smiled because things had not gone astray.

1. At the beginning of the poem, how do the animals feel? _____

How do you know? _____

_____

2. How do the animals feel at the end of the poem? _____

Why? _____

3. This poem is written in **couplets**. Look at the rhyming pattern of the poem. What

do you think **couplets** means? _____

_____

_____

A

Title _____

How well did you read?
- **1** I could not read it very well.
- **2** I needed help.
- **3** I read most of it.
- **4** I read it by myself.

B

Who is the main character?

_____

List two adjectives that describe the main character.

_____

_____

C

What is the setting of the story?

_____

List three words that describe the setting. _____

_____ _____

D

Title _____

The moral of the fable is _____

_____

_____

_____ .

E

The dog's shaggy hair **concealed** its eyes. I was amazed that it didn't run into the walls when it walked!

What does the word **concealed**

mean? _____

_____

F

What story does this story remind

you of? _____

Why? _____

_____

_____

_____

G

Read the chapter titles.
1. Duck's Special Day
2. Bear Makes a Plan
3. Bear Bakes a Cake
4. Friends Buy Gifts

What do you think the book is about?

_____

_____

H

Write two events from each part of the story.
Beginning:

_____ _____

Middle:

_____ _____

End:

_____

Title _____

Would you tell your friend to read this

story? _____

Why or why not? _____

_____ **I**

How did the characters solve the

problem in the story? _____

_____

Would you have solved the problem

the same way? _____

Why or why not? _____

_____ **J**

Camping in the Mountains

Read the title. What do you think the

story will be about? _____

_____

_____ **K**

What type of rhyming pattern do you
see in the poem?

_____

List two or more pairs of rhyming
words from the poem.

_____

_____ **L**

Put the events in order.

_____ He gives the flowers to Mom for
her birthday.

_____ Dad plants seeds in the garden.

_____ Mom waters the seedlings.

_____ Dad puts the flowers in a vase.

M

Underline the examples of alliteration
you find in this poem.

The tiny turtle took a turn,

because a lesson he wanted to learn.

He saw a sassy silly snake,

who taught him to dive into the lake.

N

Write two important events from
the story. Explain why each event is
important.

1. _____

_____

2. _____

_____ **O**

Which character in the story is the

most like you? _____

Explain. _____

_____

_____

_____ **P**

✦ Show What You Know ✦
Reading: Informational Text

Read the story. Then, answer the questions.

Thank the Bugs

Some bugs can **destroy** crops by eating them. Not all bugs are bad, though. Some bugs even help us. Bees move pollen from one flower to the next. This helps flowers make seeds so that there will be more flowers the next year. Bees also produce honey. Ladybugs are another helpful bug. They eat the bugs that chew on our plants. Finally, spiders may look scary, but they are very helpful bugs. They catch flies, crickets, and moths in their webs. If you find a spider inside the house, ask an adult to help you carefully place it outside. Then, it can do its job.

1. Why did the author write this passage?
   A. to entertain the reader
   B. to inform the reader
   C. to persuade the reader

2. What do ladybugs do that is helpful?
   A. They catch flies and moths.
   B. They move pollen.
   C. They eat the bugs that chew on our plants.

3. What does the word **destroy** mean?

_____

_____

4. Read the main idea. Write three details that support the main idea.
   Main idea: Not all bugs are bad.

1. _____

2. _____

3. _____

Name _____ Date _____

✦ Show What You Know ✦
Reading: Informational Text

Read the story. Then, answer the questions.

Moving the Mail

Many years ago, the Pony Express carried mail across the United States. A young man would ride a horse from place to place. He would change horses at each place. It was a hard and long ride. It would take weeks to get a letter from one place to the next.

1. Which sentence does not describe the Pony Express?

   A. Mail was loaded on train cars and carried through the mountains.

   B. Young men carried the mail as they rode horses from place to place.

   C. It was a long, hard ride that took weeks.

2. The author says that the men would change horses at each place. Underline the sentence that tells why the men would change horses.

3. What is the main idea of the passage? _____

_____

4. How does the illustration help you understand the text?

_____

_____

Before, During, and After Reading Prompts

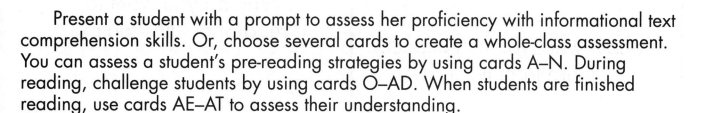

Present a student with a prompt to assess her proficiency with informational text comprehension skills. Or, choose several cards to create a whole-class assessment. You can assess a student's pre-reading strategies by using cards A–N. During reading, challenge students by using cards O–AD. When students are finished reading, use cards AE–AT to assess their understanding.

Tell two or more things you already know about the topic. Think of two or more things you would like to learn about the topic. **A**	Look at the picture. What does the picture tell you about the topic? **B**
Look over the text. Find two or more words that may not be familiar to you. Find out the meaning of each word. What do these words tell you about the topic? **C**	Read the bold words in the text. How do they help you understand the topic? **D**
Read the captions below the pictures. How do the captions and the pictures help you understand the topic before you read the text? **E**	After reading the title, write two predictions about what you will learn from reading this text. **F**

Read the first sentence. Then, read the last sentence. What do these sentences tell you about what you can expect to learn from this text?

G

Why do you want to read about this topic?

H

Copy two or more bold words from the text. Use the words in questions you write about the topic.

I

Which part of the text do you think will help you best understand the topic: the text features, the illustrations, or the text? Why?

J

Why did the author write this text?

K

What experiences from your life does this topic remind you of?

L

What are three things you expect to learn about this topic?

M

Read the subheadings. How do the subheadings help you make predictions about the text?

N

Which part of the text is not making sense to you? Write one question you have about the text.

O

Look at the picture and read the caption. How does the picture help you understand what you are reading?

P

List three or more details from the text that help you understand the topic.

Q

What is the main idea of the text? How do you know?

R

Write one or more things you have learned since you started reading the text.

S

Write a short summary of the text you have read so far.

T

Check your fluency. Is your pace too slow or too fast? Are you pausing at periods and other punctuation marks?

U

Are there any transitional words such as *first, next,* or *last* in the text? How do they help you understand what you are reading?

V

Are you eager to finish the text? Why or why not?

W

Find two words that you are unfamiliar with. Copy the words and then write the meaning of each word as it is used in the text.

X

Write a new title and subheadings for the text.

Y

What information is in the diagram? Why do you think the author put the information in a diagram instead of in the text?

Z

What is the author's point of view? How would the text be different if it was written from a different point of view?

AA

What is your opinion of what you have read so far?

AB

Draw a picture showing one thing you have learned from the text.

AC

Make a glossary for the text. Include two or more words and one or more drawings in your glossary. Add to your glossary as you keep reading the text.

AD

Read another text about the same topic. How are they the same? How are they different?

AE

What are two questions you still have about the topic? How could you find out the answers?

AF

Copy one sentence that tells you how the author feels about the topic. Do you agree with the author? Why or why not?

AG

Would you like to read another text by this author? Why or why not?

AH

How do the captions help you understand the text?

AI

Copy three words that you may not be familiar with. Write the definition of each word. Use each word in a new sentence.

AJ

Explain the fact from the text that is most interesting to you. Use details from the text to support your opinion.

AK

List three details from the text that support the main idea.

AL

Write a short summary of the text. Use *who, what, when, where,* and *why* to help you write.

AM

What are two steps you could take to learn more about the topic?

AN

Imagine that you are the author. Write three things that you want people to remember most about your text.

AO

What knowledge did you have about the topic before you started reading? Did it help you understand what you read?

AP

Pretend that one of your classmates is going to read the text for the first time. What information will you give him or her before reading to help them understand what they read?

AQ

In what order is the information presented? Would it be easier to understand if it was presented in a different order?

AR

List five adjectives that describe the topic.

AS

How does this topic relate to your life?

AT

Main Idea

Read the text. Then, answer the questions.

Communicating with Koko

Can a gorilla talk? Gorillas do not form words the way humans do. But, one gorilla, Koko, learned sign language. She talked with her hands. And, she understood what humans said.

Dr. Penny Patterson is the scientist who taught sign language to Koko. She showed Koko a picture of the two of them together. Penny pointed to Koko in the picture and asked, "Who's that?"

Koko answered by signing her own name, Koko.

1. How does Koko communicate with humans?

   A. She forms words.

   B. She uses pictures.

   C. She uses sign language.

2. What is the most important idea in the text?

   A. Koko, the gorilla, learned how to communicate with humans.

   B. Dr. Penny Patterson showed Koko a picture of the two of them.

   C. Koko is a gorilla.

3. Do you think Koko understands Penny? _____

   Why or why not? _____

   _____

4. Write a new title for the passage. _____

5. Write a short summary of the passage.

   _____

   _____

   _____

Determining the Meanings of Words

Read the text. Then, answer the questions.

Watch the Weather!

Weather can be wonderful or very **frightening**. Rain feels nice on a hot day, but too much rain can cause a flood. People can lose their cars and homes and, sometimes, their lives. A gentle breeze feels good on your skin, but a strong wind can form a tornado, or twister. A tornado can rip the roof off of a house. Snow can be fun to play in, but you cannot always travel through a snowstorm. If a news report says that the weather is going to be dangerous, do not be too **hasty** to go outside and watch. It is more fun to watch bad weather on TV than to be caught in it!

1. What does the word **frightening** mean?

_____

_____

2. What does the word **hasty** mean?

_____

_____

3. List three ways weather can be wonderful.

_____

_____

_____

4. List three ways weather can be frightening.

_____

_____

_____

Name _____ Date _____

Making the Connection between Ideas

Read the text. Then, answer the questions.

Keeping You Going

Your heart and lungs are important parts of your body. The heart moves blood through the body. Without lungs, you could not breathe. You must exercise to keep your heart and lungs healthy. Your heart starts beating faster when you run fast or jump rope. You may breathe harder too. It is good to make your heart and lungs work harder sometimes. This makes them stronger, and you will also feel healthier. Keeping yourself healthy can be a lifelong practice and can give you a long life.

1. Complete the Venn diagram with information from the text.

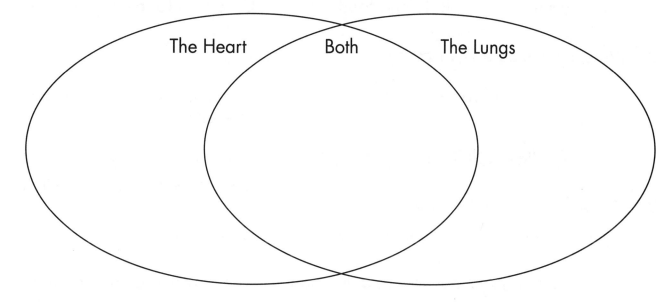

The Heart   Both   The Lungs

2. If your heart starts beating faster when you run fast, what do you think your heart does when you play soccer? Why?

_____

_____

3. Write one more question you still have about the heart or lungs.

_____

_____

Sequencing Steps

Read the text. Then, answer the questions.

A Flashy Fish

What kind of fish comes out only at night? The flashlight fish! It has a special way to stay safe. It has lights under its eyes.

How does the flashlight fish use its lights to stay safe? First, it uncovers its lights by opening its eyelid. Next, it swims in a straight line. A dangerous fish follows the lights. Then, the flashlight fish covers its lights. Last, it turns and races away. The dangerous fish cannot see where the flashlight fish went. The flashlight fish is safe.

1. How does the flashlight fish use its light?

    A. to stay safe   B. to find food   C. to hunt for other fish

2. Write the numbers 1–4 to show the correct order.

    _____ It turns and races away.   _____ It uncovers its lights by opening its eyelid.

    _____ The flashlight fish covers its lights. _____ It swims in a straight line. A dangerous fish follows the lights.

3. Where are the flashlight fish's lights?

    A. near its tail   B. under its eyes   C. in its fins

4. If a flashlight fish was not named a flashlight fish, what would be a good name for it? _____

    Why? _____

5. Pretend that your friend wants to read this passage. He talks to you before he reads it. What will you tell him that will help him better understand the text?

_____

_____

_____

Name _____ Date _____

Cause and Effect

Read the text. Then, answer the questions.

Your Community

A community is a group of people who care about each other. A community might **include** your neighbors, school, sports teams, or clubs. People will often offer to help others in their communities. You can be useful to each other. You might decide to walk your neighbor's dog or go to the store for your grandmother. Your uncle might watch your cat while your family goes on vacation. A family down the street might ask you if you want to go to the movies. It is important for people to feel like part of a community. Many people volunteer to work in their communities.

1. What does the word **include** mean? _____

_____

Use the word in a new sentence.

_____

2. Match each cause to its effect.

_____ 1. Because people care for each other,

_____ 2. While your family goes on vacation,

_____ 3. Because it is important for people to feel like part of a community,

A. your uncle might watch your cat.

B. many people volunteer to work in their communities.

C. they offer to help each other.

3. Write three benefits of living in a community. _____

_____

_____

_____

Name _____ Date _____

Using Text Features

Read the text. Then, answer the questions.

Interesting Insects

All insects have six legs. Butterflies and bees have six legs. They are insects. Spiders have eight legs. They are not insects.

What's on the Menu?

Different insects eat different things. Some insects eat plants. Caterpillars eat leaves. Bees and butterflies like the nectar of flowers. Some insects eat other insects. Ladybugs eat aphids.

Home, Sweet Home

Insects live in different kinds of homes. Bees build hives from wax. Ants and termites build hills on the ground. Some insects like mayflies and damselflies spend most of their lives underwater. Others live under rocks or in old logs.

1. Where would you look for information about a damselfly's home?

   A. paragraph 1   B. paragraph 2   C. paragraph 3

2. Circle the subheadings in the text above.

3. How is the information in the first paragraph similar to the information in the second paragraph? _____

   _____

   How is the information in the first paragraph different from the information in the second paragraph? _____

   _____

4. Write the main idea of the third paragraph. _____

   _____

   List a detail that supports the main idea.

   _____

A

Title _____

How well did you read?

1 I could not read it very well.

2 I needed help.

3 I read most of it.

4 I read it by myself.

B

Habitats

Desert Habitat 5
Wetlands Habitat...................14
Forest Habitat.......................22
Grassland Habitat.................29

How does a table of contents help you make predictions about the text?

_____

C

Complete the table.

Main Idea	
Supporting Detail	Supporting Detail

D

List the steps in the order they are presented in the text.

1. _____

2. _____

3. _____

4. _____

E

Read two nonfiction texts on the same topic.

How are the two texts alike?

_____

How are they different?

_____

F

Cross out the detail that should not be included in this nonfiction passage.

Title: Teeth Change as You Grow

A. When you are a child, you have baby teeth.

B. When you are an adult, you will have 32 teeth.

C. The Tooth Fairy wears pink dresses.

G

Write two questions you still have about the topic.

_____

_____

Where can you look for answers?

_____

_____

H

How do the bold words help you understand what you are reading?

_____

_____

Write one bold word and then write its meaning.

_____

_____

What is the author's point of view?

_____

_____

How do you know?

_____

_____

I

Why do you think the author wrote this text?

_____

_____

_____

_____

J

Read the text. Underline the main idea.
Seeds move from one place to another. Sometimes, people plant seeds. Sometimes, seeds attach to the fur of animals. Sometimes, the wind blows the seeds. Sometimes, seeds float in the water.

K

Record three words from the glossary. Beside each word, write its meaning.

_____

_____

_____

_____

L

If you could talk to the author about the text, what two things would you tell him or her you learned?

_____

_____

_____

_____

M

Look at the chart. Write a question you could ask about the chart.

Person	Monday	Wednesday
Kevin	laundry	dusting
Sara	dusting	laundry

_____

_____

N

Which part of the text does not make sense to you? How can you make it easier to understand?

_____

_____

_____

_____

O

Write a short summary of the text. Use words like *first*, *next*, *then*, and *last* as you write the steps from the text.

_____

_____

_____

_____

P

✦ Show What You Know ✦
Reading: Foundational Skills

Read each word aloud. Write **L** if the word has a long vowel sound. Write **S** if the word has a short vowel sound.

1. ___ might   ___ stain   ___ peep   ___ stem   ___ throw

2. ___ slid   ___ stamp   ___ beach   ___ soap   ___ stop

3. Write the long *i* word that matches each clue.

the opposite of dark _____   to fasten with a string _____

4. Write the long *a* word that matches each clue.

water that falls from the sky _____   opposite of leave _____

5. Write the long *e* word that matches each clue.

opposite of dirty _____

mixture of blue and yellow _____

6. Write the long *o* word that matches each clue.

a small ship _____   a black bird _____

Cross out the nonsense word in each group.

7. peel   teep   deer   **8.** spray   gray   qay

9. fow   slow   row   **10.** stight   fight   high

Unscramble each set of letters to form a two-syllable word with a long vowel sound.

11. eblta _____   **12.** smcui _____

13. tliesn _____   **14.** aelxr _____

✦ Show What You Know ✦
Reading: Foundational Skills

Read each word aloud. Write **L** if the word has a long vowel sound. Write **S** if the word has a short vowel sound.

1. ___ edge   ___ night   ___ meal   ___ mint   ___ toad

2. ___ play   ___ black   ___ stick   ___ clock   ___ crow

3. Write the long *i* word that matches each clue.

held firmly in place __ __ __ __ __   dessert with crust and fruit __ __ __

4. Write the long *a* word that matches each clue.

stay in one place __ __ __ __   mix black and white __ __ __ __

5. Write the long *e* word that matches each clue.

lunch or dinner __ __ __ __   wife of the king __ __ __ __ __

6. Write the long *o* word that matches each clue.

person who trains the team __ __ __ __ __ __

not fast __ __ __ __

Cross out the nonsense word in each row.

7. pail   laim   wait   **8.** lie   die   mie

9. soam   goal   toast   **10.** beat   heal   veat

Unscramble each set of letters to form a two-syllable word with a long vowel sound.

11. seetrc __ __ __ __ __ __   **12.** nogbel __ __ __ __ __ __

13. raepp __ __ __ __ __   **14.** tleoh __ __ __ __ __

Word Lists

DECODING WORDS

Use these lists of words when you are assessing language concepts. The lists are not comprehensive but can be used as grade-level examples for creating your own assessments, flash cards, etc.

Short Vowels

a
back
fast
flag
hand

e
dress
neck
smell
then

i
gift
miss
skip
stick

o
block
drop
rock
stop

u
dust
pump
stuck
stump

Long Vowels with Silent *e*

a
make
plane
same
wave

e
delete
eve
theme
these

i
bite
ripe
time
wide

o
home
hope
joke
vote

u
cute
fume
huge
mute

Long Vowel Digraphs

ai
chain
fail
pail
rain
wait

ay
day
gray
spray
stay
way

ea
beach
clean
heal
peach
seal

ee
green
jeep
need
queen
sheep

ie /e/
believe
brief
chief
thief

ie /i/
die
lie
pie
tie

igh
fright
high
knight
sight

oa
coast
float
load
moan
toad

ow
flown
known
mow
slow
throw

Word Lists

R-Controlled Vowels

ar
arm
barn
card
farm
jar

er
germ
kernel
nerve
serve
verse

ir
bird
circle
dirt
girl
swirl

or
fork
horse
morning
sport
worn

ur
blur
curl
nurse
turkey
turtle

Dipthongs

au
auto
autumn
daughter
sauce
taught

aw
claw
crawl
draw
hawk
lawn

oi
coin
foil
joint
spoil
voice

oy
boy
employ
joy
loyal
toy

ou
about
cloud
noun
round
shout

ow
brown
crowd
gown
how
power

/oo/ as in book
cook
good
foot
soot
wood

/oo/ as in cool
broom
moon
pool
root
soon

Initial Digraphs

ch
chair
cheese
chip

ph
phase
phone
photo

sh
shade
short
show

th
thank
thing
thumb

wh
whale
wheel
white

Ending Digraphs

ch
coach
each
much

ck
back
duck
sick

sh
cash
dish
push

th
bath
tooth
truth

Nonsense Words
besh
daw
dem
gar
loat
lork
mib
morg
pab
sug
swick
tob

October in the Orchard

One crisp morning in October, we drove to the mountains to pick apples. We took Daddy's old pickup truck. When we got to the orchard, we spied hundreds of trees filled with apples! Some were golden yellow, and some were bright red. We even saw some that were green. I took a bite from one of the apples. It tasted so sweet. The juice **dribbled** down my chin. We picked three bushels of apples. Then, we went home to bake some pies.

October in the Orchard

One crisp morning in October, we drove to the mountains to pick	12
apples. We took Daddy's old pickup truck. When we got to the orchard,	25
we spied hundreds of trees filled with apples! Some were golden yellow,	37
and some were bright red. We even saw some that were green. I took a	52
bite from one of the apples. It tasted so sweet. The juice dribbled down	66
my chin. We picked three bushels of apples. Then, we went home to bake	80
some pies.	82

Number of Words Read	Words per Minute	Words Read in Error
First Try		
Second Try		
Third Try		

A Group Game

Have you ever played charades? Charades is a fun game to play with a large group of friends. All you need to play is a pencil and paper.

Split the group into two teams. Each team writes down book, movie, and song titles on little pieces of paper. The pieces of paper are then put into two bowls. One person takes a piece of paper from the other team's bowl. That person must act out the title. Her team has to guess what the title is.

First, the player shows the team whether it is a movie, song, or book. The player cannot talk or make sounds. Only hand and body motions are allowed. The player shows how many words are in the title. Then, the team watches the player act out the words. They guess and shout out their answers. Everyone gets a turn. Both teams play. The winner is the team that guesses the most titles.

A Group Game

Have you ever played charades? Charades is a fun game to play with a   14

large group of friends. All you need to play is a pencil and paper.   28

Split the group into two teams. Each team writes down book, movie, and   41

song titles on little pieces of paper. The pieces of paper are then put into two   57

bowls. One person takes a piece of paper from the other team's bowl. That   71

person must act out the title. Her team has to guess what the title is.   86

First, the player shows the team whether it is a movie, song, or book.   100

The player cannot talk or make sounds. Only hand and body motions are   113

allowed. The player shows how many words are in the title. Then, the team   127

watches the player act out the words. They guess and shout out their answers.   141

Everyone gets a turn. Both teams play. The winner is the team that guesses   155

the most titles.   158

Number of Words Read	Words per Minute	Words Read in Error
First Try		
Second Try		
Third Try		

A Fright in the Night

Josh heard something outside in the woods. It was still dark. Ma and Pa were sleeping. Josh lit the candle by his bed. There were no windows in the little cabin. Josh got up and looked out the front door. Little dark eyes looked back at him. The little dark eyes were part of a great big furry face. Josh saw the eyes rise. He saw that the eyes were part of something tall when it stood on its two legs. "Grrr . . ." growled the eyes.

Slam! Josh shut the door. He put the big wooden bar across it. He ran over to the bed and shook his father. "Pa!" he shouted. "Wake up!" He was too scared to say anything else.

Josh heard something outside in the woods. It was still dark. Ma and	13
Pa were sleeping. Josh lit the candle by his bed. There were no windows	27
in the little cabin. Josh got up and looked out the front door. Little dark eyes	43
looked back at him. The little dark eyes were part of a great big furry face.	59
Josh saw the eyes rise. He saw that the eyes were part of something tall	74
when it stood on its two legs. "Grrr . . ." growled the eyes.	85

Slam! Josh shut the door. He put the big wooden bar across it. He ran   100

over to the bed and shook his father. "Pa!" he shouted. "Wake up!" He was   115

too scared to say anything else.   121

Number of Words Read	Words per Minute	Words Read in Error
First Try		
Second Try		
Third Try		

Go with the Snow!

What sport can make you feel like you are flying? Try snowboarding. It's a little like surfing. It's a little like skateboarding. It's a little like skiing too. To snowboard, you stand on one board and glide down a snowy hill very quickly. A snowboard is shaped kind of like a skateboard, but it is longer and wider. It does not have wheels. It is made of fiberglass, wood, and metal. Snowboards come in many shapes, sizes, and colors. A beginner usually uses a short, wide board.

Snowboarders wear special boots that snap onto the snowboard. Most people ride with their left feet in front. Their toes point in a little. You can turn the board by leaning on your toes or heels. Turning on a snowboard is called edging.

Like any new sport, snowboarding takes a lot of practice. Many ski resorts allow people to snowboard on their slopes. But before they do, snowboarders must learn safety tips and rules.

Expert snowboarders can do special tricks. These people are very skilled. They are not beginners. They can ride backward. They can spin or do a wheelie, an ollie, or a grab. There are many tricks, but some experts only want to go fast down a mountain.

Go with the Snow!

What sport can make you feel like you are flying? Try snowboarding.   12

It's a little like surfing. It's a little like skateboarding. It's a little like skiing   27

too. To snowboard, you stand on one board and glide down a snowy hill   41

very quickly. A snowboard is shaped kind of like a skateboard, but it is   55

longer and wider. It does not have wheels. It is made of fiberglass, wood,   69

and metal. Snowboards come in many shapes, sizes, and colors. A   80

beginner usually uses a short, wide board.   87

Snowboarders wear special boots that snap onto the snowboard. Most   97

people ride with their left feet in front. Their toes point in a little. You can   113

turn the board by leaning on your toes or heels. Turning on a snowboard is   128

called edging.   130

Like any new sport, snowboarding takes a lot of practice. Many ski   142

resorts allow people to snowboard on their slopes. But before they do,   154

snowboarders must learn safety tips and rules.   161

Expert snowboarders can do special tricks. These people are very   171

skilled. They are not beginners. They can ride backward. They can spin or   184

do a wheelie, an ollie, or a grab. There are many tricks, but some experts   199

only want to go fast down a mountain.   207

Number of Words Read	Words per Minute	Words Read in Error
First Try		
Second Try		
Third Try		

Name _____ Date _____

Fluency Passages: Comprehension Questions

October in the Orchard (pages 45 and 46)

1. What color are the apples?

2. What does the word **dribbled** mean?

3. Could this story really happen? Why or why not?

4. Who is telling the story? How do you know?

A Group Game (pages 47 and 48)

1. What are the directions for?

2. What materials do you need to play the game?

3. What three types of titles do you write?

4. Would you want to play charades? Why or why not?

A Fright in the Night (pages 49 and 50)

1. Does this story take place in the past, the present, or the future?
How do you know?

2. List three adjectives from the story.

3. What do you think is standing at Josh's front door? Explain your answer.

4. What do you think will happen next?

Go with the Snow! (pages 51 and 52)

1. What equipment do snowboarders need?

2. List three sports that are like snowboarding.

3. Name at least two tricks that snowboarders can learn to do.

4. Would you like to try snowboarding? Why or why not?

A

Read each word aloud. Circle each word that has a long vowel sound.

beat	dress
braid	known
pump	chief
vote	sheep
flag	dust

B

Read each word aloud. Circle each word that has a short vowel sound.

sigh	fell
frog	gift
smoke	plane
hand	cube
hug	bend

C

Write the long *a* words.

1. a large body of water

_ _ _ _ _ _

2. water from the sky _ _ _ _ _ _ _

3. the month after April _ _ _ _ _

4. not shy _ _ _ _ _ _ _

D

Write the long *e* words.

1. a bird's mouth _ _ _ _ _ _

2. a tall plant with a trunk

_ _ _ _ _ _

3. a fish-eating mammal _ _ _ _ _ _ _

4. a farm animal _ _ _ _ _ _ _

E

Write the long *i* words.

1. not low _ _ _ _ _ _

2. to stop living _ _ _ _ _

3. not narrow _ _ _ _ _ _

4. not dim _ _ _ _ _ _ _

F

Write the long *o* words.

1. a street or path _ _ _ _ _ _

2. frozen rain _ _ _ _ _ _

3. a riddle _ _ _ _ _ _

4. a house _ _ _ _ _

G

Write the long *u* words.

1. really large _ _ _ _ _ _

2. an animal like a donkey

_ _ _ _ _

3. a 3-D shape _ _ _ _ _ _

4. to put into service _ _ _ _ _ _

H

Unscramble each set of letters to make a two-syllable word with a long-vowel sound.

1. knebor _____

2. despri _____

3. doybne _____

4. lfbea _____

Writing Prompts

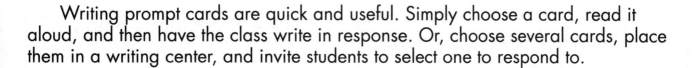

Writing prompt cards are quick and useful. Simply choose a card, read it aloud, and then have the class write in response. Or, choose several cards, place them in a writing center, and invite students to select one to respond to.

Pretend that you are going on vacation. Think about where you are going and what you will see. Write a story about your trip. **A**	Imagine that you can live on the bottom of the ocean. Would you? Why or why not? **B**
Imagine that you are walking in the jungle and you meet a talking monkey. Write a story about the conversation you have with the monkey. **C**	What if electricity had never been invented? Write a story about how you would live one day with no electricity. **D**
You have been asked to spend a day helping the zookeeper! What job would you like to do at the zoo? Write a story about the day you spend working at the zoo. **E**	Pretend that you are walking down a street when you see a bear driving a car! What happens next? **F**

Imagine that one of the cooks calls you into the kitchen. She tells you to walk quietly while she slowly lifts the pot lid. You lean over and see . . .

G

Write a story titled "The Day I Found the End of the Rainbow."

H

Write a story titled "The Day They Forgot to Open the School."

I

Pretend that you own your own restaurant. Write a menu for your restaurant. Describe the foods so that people will want to order them.

J

Plan the best birthday party you can imagine. Write a story about this amazing birthday party.

K

Write a letter to your principal. Describe one thing that you really like about your school. Describe one thing that you would like to change about your school.

L

Write a letter to your teacher. Tell your teacher five or more things you would like to learn before the school year is over.

M

Write a letter to a friend. Tell your friend about the best book you have ever read. Convince your friend that he should read the book too.

N

Imagine you meet a genie who tells you that he will give you one wish, either a million dollars or a million friends. Write a paragraph to tell which you will choose and why.

O

Which animal makes the best pet? Write a paragraph explaining your choice.

P

Write about a new toy you have invented. Describe the toy and convince other kids to want to play with this toy too.

Q

Would you rather get a very large present or a very small present? Write a paragraph explaining your choice.

R

Write a story describing three things you can do in the summer that you cannot do in the winter.

S

Write a description of the best gift you have ever given to someone else. Why did you give that person the gift?

T

Are you the same person you were when you started kindergarten? Describe three ways you are different. Describe three ways you are the same.

U

Make a list of all of the things that make you smile. Write a paragraph describing these things.

V

Finish this sentence in at least ten different ways: *On hot summer days, I love to . . .*

W

Write a summary of the rules for your favorite game. Use transition words like *first*, *next*, *then*, and *last* in your summary.

X

Write about a time when you tried to learn something new. Who taught you this new skill? How hard or easy was it to learn?

Y

What topic would you like to know more about? Write three questions you have about the topic. Do research to find the answers and then write a paragraph about your research.

Z

Write a list of rhyming words. Then, use the words to write a silly poem.

AA

Write a poem about your favorite food. Label the rhyming pattern in your poem.

AB

Make a list of adjectives that describe your favorite season. Write a poem about your favorite season using the adjectives in your list.

AC

Make a list of things that are red. Write a poem about red things.

AD

Editing for Grammar, Spelling, and Capitalization

Read the story. Underline the eight mistakes. Then, rewrite the story without any mistakes.

Around Town

After skool, my frend and i went to the park. we played soccer. We road our bikes My friend fell and hert his leg. I callt his mom for help.

_____

_____

_____

_____

_____

Read the story. Underline the seven mistakes. Then, rewrite the story without any mistakes.

Day Trip

We are walkeng to the store My sister wil meet us there. She will by some froot for us. Last we will go to the movees

_____

_____

_____

_____

_____

_____

Revising Writing

Rewrite each sentence. Replace the underlined word with a better word.

1. My friend <u>said</u>, "Hello!"

_____

2. The diamond was <u>pretty</u>.

_____

3. The dog <u>ate</u> the bone.

_____

4. My dad was <u>happy</u> when my team won.

_____

5. I like to <u>watch</u> the birds.

_____

6. She <u>ran</u> to the library.

_____

7. That dog is <u>little</u>!

_____

8. The <u>smart</u> boy won the game.

_____

9. How many <u>things</u> are in the bag?

_____

10. She was <u>mad</u> when it broke.

_____

Read the story. Circle the four mistakes.

the flowers smell good. the red ones are my favorite Next year, I hop we plant some more.

A

Read the story. Circle the five mistakes.

Yesterday i was walk on the street My friend stoped me. he gave me a new game!

B

Read the story. Circle the five mistakes.

i see the bird. that bird is flying hi It is above the treez.

C

Read the story. Circle the six mistakes.

We are painting my room The paint is blew. Blew is my favorite color. Win it is don, we will paint the living room

D

Read the story. Circle the six mistakes.

my class is going to the zoo. it will be fun! i want to sea the bears. lynn wants to see the shark tank

E

Read each main idea. Cross out the detail that does not belong.

baseball
glove
uniform
tooth
bat

space
moon
cricket
stars
planets

F

Read each main idea. Cross out the detail that does not belong.

pets
bird
dog
bike
kitten

clothes
pants
shirts
socks
dog

G

Read each main idea. Cross out the detail that does not belong.

picnic
ants
brush
tablecloth
food

cooking
pots
pans
vacuum
spoon
stove

H

Unscramble each set of letters to make a two-syllable word with a long vowel sound.

1. poanr _____

2. snuob _____

3. letoh _____

4. agnbe _____

I

Unscramble each set of letters to make a two-syllable word with a long vowel sound.

1. dracle _____

2. nleao _____

3. spyeel _____

4. dlay _____

J

Unscramble each set of letters to make a word with a long *a* sound.

1. ryasp _____

2. tinaf _____

3. ilsna _____

4. aryg _____

K

Unscramble each set of letters to make a word with a long *e* sound.

1. twahe _____

2. enek _____

3. eeds _____

4. anelc _____

L

Unscramble each set of letters to make a word with a long *i* sound.

1. hitgm _____

2. ile _____

3. ghist _____

4. htikgn _____

M

Unscramble each set of letters to make a word with a long *o* sound.

1. rwhot _____

2. scaot _____

3. wlfno _____

4. raong _____

N

Replace the underlined word with a better word.

1. The <u>big</u> dog scared the kids.

_____

2. The cake tastes <u>great</u>!

_____

O

Replace the underlined word with a better word.

1. The fair was <u>cool</u>. _____

2. The show made us <u>laugh</u>.

_____

3. I <u>like</u> cats. _____

P

Name _____ Date _____

Show What You Know
Conventions

Read each sentence. Write the plural of the underlined noun on the line in the second sentence.

1. She went to the store to buy a <u>dress</u>.

She tried three _____ on before she bought one.

2. She loves to play at the <u>park</u>.

There are lots of _____ in the city.

Circle the collective noun in each sentence.

3. The colony of ants crawled onto the picnic blanket.

4. We saw a troop of apes in the zoo.

Circle the correct plural noun for each noun.

5. die   dice   dies   dices

6. wife   wifes   wives   wifess

Rewrite the sentence with the correct form of the possessive noun.

7. The **dog** that belongs to my **brother** is in the house.

_____

Write the correct reflexive pronoun using **herself**, **myself**, or **themselves**.

8. I like to walk to school by _____ .

9. The girls can bake the cookies by _____ .

10. Mary lost _____ in the great book she was reading.

Circle the action verb in each sentence.

11. Tom talked to the teacher after school.

12. My mother goes to work on Mondays.

Write the correct past tense verb on the line.

13. All of my friends _____ to my party. (come, came)

14. The sun _____ over the mountains. (risen, rose)

Underline the adjectives.

15. There is a large spider! It has eight hairy legs!

16. We ordered two pizzas. They are hot and cheesy.

Underline the adverbs.

17. The boys ran quickly. Then, they stopped carefully.

18. My socks are inside the drawer. I can find them easily.

Combine the sentences to make one sentence. Write the sentence on the line.

19. Tracy walked to the zoo. Fred walked to the zoo.

_____

20. We baked cupcakes. We baked cookies.

_____

Circle each letter that should be capitalized.

21. sue is planning to spend a week in hawaii this summer.

22. nick gave a bouquet of flowers to his mother on valentine's day.

Insert commas where needed.

23. January 31 2018

24. I want to visit Houston Texas.

25. My sister likes to skate cook and read.

Write a contraction on the line to complete the sentence.

26. _____ on my way to the library.
    I am

Show What You Know
Conventions

Read each sentence. Write the plural of the underlined noun on the line in the second sentence.

1. He carried the <u>box</u> down the stairs.

He put it next to the other _____.

2. The <u>light</u> was very bright.

He turned the _____ off so he could sleep.

Circle the collective noun in each sentence.

3. Mike drew a picture of a caravan of camels.

4. The rabbit was hiding in the forest of trees.

Circle the correct plural for each noun.

5. man   men   mans   mens

6. moose   mooses   meese   moose

Rewrite the sentence with the correct form of the possessive noun.

7. Where is the **doll** of my **sister**? _____

Write the correct reflexive pronoun using **yourselves**, **himself**, or **ourselves**.

8. He can clean his room by _____ .

9. Would you two like to go to the movie by _____ ?

10. We are going to walk home by _____ .

Circle the action verb in each sentence.

11. Rob pulled the wagon to the store.

12. Alice swam across the pool.

Write the correct past tense verb on the line.

13. My sister _____ the bracelet I lost. (found, finded)

14. Dad _____ more pancakes on my plate. (putted, put)

Underline the adjectives.

15. The cold air made me shiver. The icy wind made my toes turn blue.

16. Dad cooked spicy tacos. The hot meat burned my tongue.

Underline the adverbs.

17. The waterfall crashed loudly. It splashed as we walked nearby.

18. We often listen to the radio. We always like the commercials.

Combine the sentences to make one sentence. Write the sentence on the line.

19. She washed the dishes. She washed the clothes.

_____

20. A fish swam in the pond. A turtle swam in the pond.

_____

Circle each word that should be capitalized.

21. mark buys his christmas presents in november.

22. We like to visit the miller city zoo on tuesdays.

Insert commas where needed.

23. September 13 2017

24. My favorite colors are green pink and purple.

25. I live in Smithtown Ohio.

Write a contraction on the line to finish the sentence.

26. _____ ride her bicycle to my house today.
        She will

✦ Show What You Know ✦
Language

Read each word. Draw a line between each prefix and the root word.

1. unhappy   **2.** bicycle

3. rebuild   **4.** preschool

Write the meaning of each word.

5. rebuild _____

6. unhappy _____

Read each word. Draw a line between each root word and the suffix.

7. worthless   **8.** graceful

9. gardener   **10.** loveless

Write the meaning of each word.

11. graceful _____

12. gardener _____

Write the compound word that completes each sentence.

13. A pot that holds flowers is a _____ .

14. A chair with wheels on it is a _____ .

Circle the correct meaning of the underlined word. Use the context clues to help you.

15. Erin can only eat the corn and the salad because she is a <u>vegetarian</u>.

   A. a person from Venezuela

   B. a person who only eats vegetables, fruits, nuts, and grains

   C. a person who reads about salads

✦ Show What You Know
Language

Read each word. Draw a line between each prefix and the root word.

1. r e w r i t e   **2.** p r e p a y

3. u n p a c k   **4.** b i w e e k l y

Write the meaning of each word.

5. prepay _____

6. rewrite _____

Read each word. Draw a line between each root word and the suffix.

7. t e a c h e r   **8.** p r i c e l e s s

9. t r u t h f u l   **10.** h o p e f u l

Write the meaning of each word.

11. priceless _____

12. hopeful _____

Write the compound word that completes each sentence.

13. A box full of sand is a _____ .

14. A paper filled with news is a _____ .

Circle the correct meaning of the underlined word. Use the context clues to help you.

15. Peter loves to <u>recite</u> poetry in front of his classmates, especially if he has memorized the poem before he repeats it to the class.

   A. do a live dance

   B. call again; tell over

   C. tell from memory; present in a formal way

Word Lists

PARTS OF SPEECH

Use these lists of words when you are assessing language concepts. The lists are not comprehensive but can be used as grade-level examples for creating your own assessments, flash cards, etc.

IRREGULAR PLURAL NOUNS

Singular Reflexive Pronouns
herself
himself
itself
myself
yourself

Plural Reflexive Pronouns
ourselves
themselves
yourselves

Collective Nouns
bouquet (flowers)
caravan (camels)
clan (hyenas)
clutch (chicks, eggs)
colony (ants, bats, beavers)
convoy (trucks)
deck (cards)
den (snakes)
fleet (ships)
forest (trees)
hive (bees)
litter (kittens, puppies)
pack (wolves)
pride (lions)
troop (apes)

Words That Change the *f* to *v* and Add *-es*
half/halves
loaf/loaves
shelf/shelves
wife/wives
wolf/wolves

Words That Change Spelling
child/children
die/dice
foot/feet
goose/geese
man/men
mouse/mice
ox/oxen
person/people
woman/women

Words That Don't Change Spelling
deer
moose
sheep
shrimp

IRREGULAR VERBS

Infinitive	Simple Past	Past Participle
be	was/were	been
begin	began	begun
bring	brought	brought
build	built	built
buy	bought	bought
choose	chose	chosen
come	came	come
do	did	done
drive	drove	driven
eat	ate	eaten
fall	fell	fallen
find	found	found
freeze	froze	frozen
get	got	got
give	gave	given
go	went	gone
have	had	had
hide	hid	hidden
hurt	hurt	hurt
know	knew	known
leave	left	left
light	lit	lit
meet	met	met
pay	paid	paid
read	read	read
rise	rose	risen
see	saw	seen
shut	shut	shut
sleep	slept	slept
speak	spoke	spoken
take	took	taken
tell	told	told
write	wrote	written

Word Lists

VOCABULARY

Prefixes

bi- (two)
biceps
bicycle
biweekly

dis- (not, opposite of)
disagree
disconnect
dislike

mis- (wrongly)
misinterpret
misprint
misspell

non- (not, opposite of)
nondairy
nonfat
nonfiction

pre- (before)
preschool
pretest
preview

re- (again, back)
redo
remake
reread

un- (not, opposite of)
unable
unsafe
untie

under- (too little, below)
underarm
underground
underwater

Suffixes

-ed (past tense)
barked
fixed
worked

-er (someone who)
baker
farmer
teacher

-ful (full of)
graceful
hopeful
truthful

-less (without)
clueless
sleepless
timeless

-ly (characteristic of)
angrily
kindly
sweetly

-y (characterized by)
bony
cloudy
scary

Compound Words

airplane
anybody
applesauce
basketball
baseball
bedroom
birdhouse
birthday
butterfly
classmate
cowboy
crosswalk
daylight
downstairs
driveway
earrings
eggshell
everybody
fingernail
flagpole
flowerpot
football
gingerbread
goldfish
grandfather
grandmother
grasshopper
hamburger
highway
homework
indoors
jellyfish
keyboard

lifeguard
lighthouse
mailbox
motorcycle
newspaper
nighttime
notebook
oatmeal
outside
paintbrush
pancake
playground
popcorn
railroad
rainbow
rattlesnake
sailboat
scarecrow
seashell
spaceship
starfish
strawberry
suitcase
teammate
upstairs
warehouse
underground
underwater
warehouse
watermelon
wheelchair
windmill
windshield
woodpecker

Plural Nouns

Read each sentence. Write the plural of the underlined noun on the line in the second sentence.

1. Each <u>parent</u> is invited to Open House.

The _____ will be here on Thursday night.

2. My <u>class</u> is doing a play.

Several other _____ will be performing too.

3. Our <u>teacher</u> is very excited.

All of the _____ want to meet the parents.

4. Each student made a small <u>gift</u> for his parents.

The _____ will be in the classrooms.

5. There is a large welcome <u>poster</u> in the hallway.

There are more _____ in the gym.

6. A <u>clown</u> is giving balloons to children.

Other _____ are selling popcorn.

7. The popcorn costs one dollar a <u>box</u>.

Each family buys several _____ .

8. The librarian is reading a <u>book</u> about friends.

Children can check out _____ until 7:00.

9. The coach is giving a talk about the next field <u>trip</u>.

There will be more information about other field _____ too!

10. Everyone has fun on Open House <u>night</u>.

Students and parents look forward to _____ like these.

Name _____ Date _____

Collective Nouns

Circle the collective noun in each sentence.

1. Mary gave her mother a bouquet of flowers.

2. The den of snakes looks very scary!

3. Do not disturb that hive of bees!

4. The cat was feeding her litter of kittens.

5. There was a pack of wolves deep inside the cave.

6. Jack shuffled the deck of cards.

7. We saw a clan of hyenas at the zoo.

8. A flock of seagulls flew over the ocean.

9. We watched a school of fish swim below the pier.

10. A herd of antelope ran across the prairie.

Write two sentences. Use a collective noun in each one. Use the collective nouns in the box to help you.

deck	school	bouquet
herd	pack	den

11. _____

_____

12. _____

_____

Irregular Plural Nouns

Circle the correct plural for each noun.

1.	ox	oxes	oxen	ox
2.	wolf	wolves	wolfs	wolfes
3.	sheep	sheep	sheeps	sheepes
4.	person	persons	peoples	people
5.	wife	wifes	wivies	wives
6.	foot	feet	foots	feets
7.	deer	deers	deer	deers
8.	loaf	loaves	loafs	loafes
9.	goose	gooses	geeses	geese
10.	woman	women	womans	womens
11.	half	halfes	halves	halfs
12.	child	childs	child	children

If the noun is plural, write **P**. If the noun is singular, write **S**.

_____ **13.** knife   _____ **14.** geese   _____ **15.** wolves

_____ **16.** ox   _____ **17.** people   _____ **18.** child

_____ **19.** loaves   _____ **20.** foot   _____ **21.** men

Reflexive Pronouns

Write the correct reflexive pronoun on each line. Use the words in the box to help you. Some words may be used more than once.

herself	**himself**	**itself**
myself	**ourselves**	**themselves**
yourself	**yourselves**	

1. The dog can jump on the sofa by _____ .

2. I hurt _____ when I tripped over the cord.

3. The girls like to see _____ in the mirror.

4. Can you paint the room by _____ ?

5. We like to bake cookies by _____ .

6. The boy bought a new shirt by _____ .

7. You kids will enjoy _____ if you go to the party.

8. Mary behaved _____ at school today.

9. At school, we like to do things by _____ .

10. Matt's dad carefully shaves _____ .

11. The spider spun the web by _____ .

12. I am very proud of _____ !

Name _____ Date _____

Identifying Verbs

Circle the action verb in each sentence. Then, rewrite the sentence with a new action verb.

1. The officer walks around the park.

_____

2. Leo dances in the rain.

_____

3. The children play in the park.

_____

4. My mother saw a rainbow.

_____

5. The cars moved quickly on the road.

_____

6. Carrie left school early.

_____

7. Jane jumped in the puddle.

_____

8. The monkey threw the ball.

_____

Past Tense Verbs

Write the correct past tense verb on the line.

1. We _____ a package in the mail yesterday. (getted, got)

2. I _____ a picture of a giraffe. (drew, drawed)

3. My sister fell and _____ her arm. (hurt, hurted)

4. Michael _____ all of the pizza! (eated, ate)

5. My teacher let us _____ our new seats. (choosed, choose)

6. The plants _____ during the snowstorm. (froze, frozed)

7. We _____ for the books before we read them. (payed, paid)

8. The girls _____ their best dresses to the meeting. (wears, wore)

9. Mom _____ the door quickly. (shut, shutted)

10. All of the leaves _____ off the tree. (fell, fallen)

11. When I threw the ball, Dad _____ it. (catched, caught)

12. The teacher _____ loudly. (speaked, spoke)

Name _____ Date _____

Adjectives and Adverbs

Solve the puzzle. Use the clues below.

Across
Circle the adjective in each sentence. Then, write the adjective in the puzzle by the correct number.
1. She loves her striped sweater.
4. Mom tasted the hot food.
5. She laughed at the silly clown.
6. We planted one flower.
7. The sleepy mouse yawned.

Down
Circle the adverb in each sentence. Then, write the adverb in the puzzle by the correct number.
1. The fish swam smoothly.
2. We exercise daily.
3. The turtle crawled below the rock.
6. Lee often plays the piano.

Identifying Parts of Speech

Look at the underlined word in each sentence.
If the word names a noun, write **N**.
If the word names a verb, write **V**.
If the word names an adjective, write **A**.
If the word names an adverb, write **AV**.

_____ **1.** The dolphin swam <u>under</u> the water.

_____ **2.** There are <u>three</u> cartons of milk in the cooler.

_____ **3.** My <u>sister</u> is dancing on the stage.

_____ **4.** We liked the <u>colorful</u> garden.

_____ **5.** The baby <u>crawled</u> across the floor.

_____ **6.** The small <u>skunk</u> scurried away.

_____ **7.** Evan <u>ran</u> home after school.

_____ **8.** Will <u>carefully</u> stepped over the gate.

_____ **9.** There are three <u>pears</u> in the bowl.

_____ **10.** That <u>funny</u> dog is barking again!

_____ **11.** The crowd <u>watched</u> the holiday parade.

_____ **12.** Sarah <u>sadly</u> packed her suitcase.

Name _____ Date _____

Compound Sentences

Circle the sentence that most correctly combines the two sentences.

1. The flower is yellow. The sun is yellow.
   A. The flower and the sun are yellow.
   B. The flower is yellow and the sun.
   C. The flower and sun is yellow.

2. The boy fell off his bike. He hurt his leg.
   A. The boy fell and hurt his leg on his bike.
   B. The boy hurt his leg and fell.
   C. The boy fell off his bike and hurt his leg.

3. We swam in the lake. We floated near the dock.
   A. We floated near the dock that is in the lake.
   B. We swam in the lake and floated near the dock.
   C. We swam in the lake and near the dock.

4. Ladd is at camp. Clay is at camp.
   A. Ladd is at camp and Clay is at camp.
   B. Ladd and Clay are at camp.
   C. Ladd is at camp but Clay is also at camp.

5. Anna is at the park. Luke is at the park.
   A. Anna is at the park and Luke is at the park.
   B. Anna and Luke are at the park.
   C. Anna is at the park while Luke is at the park too.

6. We ate tossed salad. We ate spaghetti.
   A. We ate tossed salad and spaghetti.
   B. We ate tossed spaghetti.
   C. We ate tossed salad and we also ate spaghetti too.

7. The girls saw a cow. The girls saw a sheep.
   A. The girls saw a cow and a sheep.
   B. The girls saw a cow and the girls saw a sheep.
   C. The girls saw a cow and then later they saw a sheep.

8. Her hair is curly. Her hair is red.
   A. Her curly, red hair is curly.
   B. Her hair is curly and it is red too.
   C. Her hair is curly and red.

Capitalization

Circle each letter that should be capitalized. Then, rewrite the sentence correctly.

1. This monday is memorial day, and we are going to the beach.

_____

_____

2. In may, eve makes cards for mother's day.

_____

_____

3. We are going to south dakota and montana in june!

_____

_____

4. we celebrate thanksgiving on a thursday in november.

_____

_____

5. we stay at pete's oceanside campground when we are in florida.

_____

_____

6. julie decorates her house for independence day in july.

_____

_____

Commas in Letters

Add the missing commas to the friendly letter.

June 3 2018

Dear Olivia

Hello! I am writing to tell you about my trip. Mom Dad and I went to see my grandmother. She lives in Tampa Florida. She used to live in Omaha Nebraska. She moved to Florida on February 21 2017. She was tired of the snow.

On the way to Florida, we stopped in Atlanta Georgia. Mom wanted to visit my aunt uncle and cousins. They had a big party for us. My aunt served pizza cake and chips. We had a lot of fun!

My grandmother was so happy to see us! She took us to the beach. We went swimming surfing and sailing. I took pictures of shells dolphins and the pier. I cannot wait to go back!

Write to me soon!

Your friend

Kathy

Contractions

Write a contraction to complete each sentence.

1. The dog _____ walk across the street.
<u>will not</u>

2. _____ your favorite color?
<u>What is</u>

3. _____ wearing the pink and white dress.
<u>She is</u>

4. I think _____ going to leave soon.
<u>we are</u>

5. I know _____ have a good time.
<u>you will</u>

6. _____ going to the carnival after school.
<u>I am</u>

7. _____ time to eat lunch.
<u>It is</u>

8. The girls _____ go to the movies with us.
<u>cannot</u>

9. _____ make some hamburgers on the grill.
<u>She will</u>

10. _____ looked everywhere for my lost backpack.
<u>I have</u>

Possessive Nouns

Rewrite each sentence with the correct form of the possessive noun.

1. The **bike** that belongs to **Polly** is yellow.

_____

2. Have you seen the **car** that belongs to my **dad**?

_____

3. The **hands** that belong to the **clock** are not moving.

_____

4. The **bone** that belongs to the **dog** is under the tree.

_____

5. Where is the **football** that belongs to **Keith**?

_____

6. The **phone** that belongs to my **sister** is broken.

_____

7. The **friend** of my **cousin** met us at the store.

_____

8. The **tail** of the **skunk** is black and white.

_____

Prefixes and Suffixes

Add the correct prefix to the word below each line to make a new word.
Write the word on the line.

1. She ripped the sofa and had to _____ it.
cover

2. Our club meets every two weeks, or _____ .
weekly

3. She is _____ of what time they will eat dinner.
certain

4. Lisa wants to _____ the movie before we see it.
view

Write the meaning of each word.

5. preread _____

6. review _____

7. untie _____

Add the correct suffix to the word below each line to make a new word.
Write the word on the line.

8. The chef is _____ when he carries hot plates and he burns his hands.
care

9. When I play ball, I like to be the _____ .
catch

10. I feel _____ when it is time for a vacation!
joy

Write the meaning of each word.

11. gardener _____

12. graceful _____

13. cordless _____

Name _____ Date _____

Compound Words

Complete each sentence with the correct compound word. Use the words in the box to help you.

beachball	**earring**	**fireplace**
fishbowl	**gumball**	**lunchbox**
nightime	**rattlesnake**	**sailboat**
	sandcastle	

1. A ring for your ear is an _____ .

2. A ball you play with on the beach is a _____ .

3. A bowl that a fish lives in is a _____ .

4. A boat that sails on the water is a _____ .

5. A box that holds your lunch is a _____ .

6. A castle that is made of sand is a _____ .

7. Any time at night is _____ .

8. A snake that rattles is a _____ .

9. A ball that is made of gum is a _____ .

10. A place where you can build a fire is a _____ .

Name _____ Date _____

Context Clues

Circle the correct meaning of the underlined word. Use the context clues to help you.

1. We were relieved to have some time off for a nice <u>vacation</u>.
   A. party with friends
   B. time away from work or school
   C. football game

2. After she leaves high school, my sister will study medicine at the <u>university</u>.
   A. a school of higher learning; a college
   B. a hospital
   C. the city park

3. Heather knew she would feel better if she told the truth, so she <u>confessed</u> that she was the one who broke the vase.
   A. to mix two colors together
   B. to be breakable
   C. to admit; to be honest

4. Many people have moved to our city, and the <u>population</u> has grown.
   A. the height of a building
   B. the number of people who live in an area
   C. a balloon that rises in the air

5. She wondered who could have left her the <u>mysterious</u> package.
   A. unknown; of puzzling origin
   B. red and blue with a bow
   C. musical

6. We thought the artist was very <u>creative</u> because she made her art out of other people's trash!
   A. green
   B. able to think of interesting ideas
   C. broken into pieces

7. They needed lots of room for an audience, so they performed the play in the school's <u>auditorium</u>.
   A. a large library
   B. a room or building for public gatherings
   C. a playground

8. The <u>tornado</u> blew through town and did a lot of damage to buildings and trees.
   A. a storm with powerful wind
   B. a hockey team
   C. a pizza restaurant

A

Write the plural form of each noun.

1. box _____
2. girl _____
3. glove _____
4. color _____
5. miss _____

B

Write the plural form of each noun.

1. car _____
2. park _____
3. brush _____
4. mess _____
5. key _____

C

Write the plural form of each noun.

1. life _____
2. self _____
3. wife _____
4. scarf _____
5. leaf _____

D

Write the plural form of each noun.

1. deer _____
2. mouse _____
3. woman _____
4. sheep _____
5. foot _____

E

Circle the collective noun in each sentence.

1. A swarm of bees flew near the top of the trash can.
2. I ate a bunch of grapes for snack.
3. There is a fresh batch of muffins in the kitchen.

F

Circle the collective noun in each sentence.

1. There is a brood of hens on on my family's farm.
2. The hungry shark watched the school of fish.
3. The pack of wolves howled at the moon.

G

Write the correct reflexive pronoun to complete each sentence.

1. We will play the game by _____.
2. The dog found its bone by _____.
3. They enjoyed _____.

H

Write the correct reflexive pronoun to complete each sentence.

1. Jenny talked quietly to _____.
2. Maria, did you draw this by _____?
3. I am reading by _____.

Circle the action verb in each sentence.
1. The astronaut floats through space.
2. The policeman walks to the school.
3. Jane stacks the blocks for the baby.
4. The teacher writes the spelling words.
5. The cat chases the mouse.

I

Write a sentence for each action verb.
1. flies _____
_____
2. smiles _____
_____
3. reads _____
_____

J

Circle the correct past-tense verb.
1. The dog (digged, dug) a hole.
2. We (hid, hided) under the table.
3. Jon (knew, know) the answers.
4. Our team (won, win) the game!

K

Circle the correct past tense verb.
1. The vase (fell, falled) off the table.
2. She (keep, kept) all of her balloons.
3. I (lost, losed) my wallet.
4. Danny (bitten, bit) into the sandwich.

L

Underline the adjective in each sentence.
1. There is a colorful bookbag in the hall.
2. We finished the birdhouse in one day.
3. A scary bug is on the window.
4. The red fox ran under the bush.

M

Underline the adverb in each sentence.
1. Julie carefully opened the envelope.
2. We are playing baseball outside.
3. Howie chewed his gum loudly.
4. They will meet at the movies tomorrow.

N

Write each word in the correct column.

| riding | doll | green |
| sleeping | tall | cat |

Nouns	Verbs	Adjectives

O

Write each word in the correct column.

| quiet | moving | climbing |
| monkey | little | theater |

Nouns	Verbs	Adjectives

P

Combine the two sentences to make one sentence.

The green balloon is in the air.
The white balloon is in the air.

_____

_____

Q

Combine the two sentences to make one sentence.

Tina wants turkey on her sandwich.
Tina wants cheese on her sandwich.

_____

_____

R

Circle each letter that should be capitalized.

1. We will be visiting iowa on sunday.

2. On may 20, stan is going home.

3. the shop is closed on tuesdays.

4. my dog's name is rusty.

S

Circle each letter that should be capitalized.

1. my birthday is in december.

2. My friend ann lives in new york.

3. our new house is on lake drive.

4. In november, we will move to utah.

T

Add commas to the letter.
Dear Frank
    How are you? I am well. I am writing from Houston Texas. I will be at your house soon!
    Love
    Paul

U

Add commas to the letter.
Dear Lisa
    Will you come to my party? It is on August 20 2018. I hope to see you!
    Your friend
    Mary

V

Write the correct contraction for each pair of words.

1. should not _____

2. she is _____

3. we have _____

4. they are _____

5. did not _____

W

Write the correct contraction for each pair of words.

1. she will _____

2. they have _____

3. it is _____

4. could not _____

5. we are _____

X

Write the correct possessive noun.
1. the **lunch** of my **teacher**

   _____

2. the **bone** of my **dog**

   _____

3. the **wing** of the **bug**

   _____ **Y**

Write the correct possessive noun.
1. the **baseball** of my **brother**

   _____

2. the **rattle** that belongs to the **baby** _____

3. the **hands** of the **clock**

   _____ **Z**

Add the correct prefix to each word.

1. to play again   _____ play

2. not able   _____ able

3. not happy   _____ happy

4. to wind again   _____ wind **AA**

Add the correct suffix to each word.

1. full of care   care _____

2. without hope   hope _____

3. full of help   help _____

4. without worth   worth _____ **AB**

Write the compound word.

1. a house for a dog _____

2. a box for your mail _____

3. a book for notes _____

4. sauce made of apples

   _____ **AC**

Write the compound word.

1. work done on the road

   _____

2. a brush for your hair

   _____

3. a place for a fire _____

4. a room with a bed _____ **AD**

Circle the meaning of the underlined word.
1. Sarah is <u>glum</u> because her team lost the game.
   A. happy   B. sad   C. sick
2. The <u>generous</u> people gave money to the poor woman.
   A. honest   B. grasshopper
   C. kind; giving **AE**

Circle the meaning of the underlined word.
1. Peter washed his <u>grubby</u> hands before dinner.
   A. dirty   B. green   C. sunny
2. Connie must <u>adapt</u> to the cold if she wants to be an ice skater.
   A. live in   B. adjust to
   C. overcome **AF**

Answer Key

Page 9
1. Grandpa; 2. Grandpa; 3. Answers will vary but should include that *knowledge* means information that you have. 4. Answers will vary but may include *hot, warm, crackling,* and *quiet.* 5. Grandpa visits schools, he talks about fire safety, he shows students his jacket, and he tells them how to stay safe. 6. The author is proud of Grandpa. We know this because the author says, "My grandpa is a hero."

Page 10
1. Grace Chang; 2. apple seeds, cottonseeds, kernel of corn; 3. Answers will vary but should include that Grace plants things and waits for them to grow. 4. Answers will vary but should include that the things Grace grows are not normal. They do amazing things such as make themselves into pie or into a sweater. 5. Answers will vary but should include that Grace is a hero who can do amazing, unreal things.

Page 17
1. Mrs. Flores cannot find her blue pen. 2. The boys find a brown fingerprint. 3. Mr. Burke does not remember where he got the pen. 4. Answers will vary.

Page 18
1. (1) Dan measured the sugar. (2) Dan scooped out some oats. (3) Dan rolled the dough into balls. (4) Dan put the baking sheet into the oven. 2. B; 3. B; Answers will vary.

Page 19
1. They are making the necklace for the Native American Fair. 2. Answers wll vary but may include that Lynette is proud of the work she is doing. She carefully shaped the beads. Then, she carved a sun into the pendant and painted it. 3. Answers will vary but may include that Jeffrey does not care about the project. He makes the pendant quickly and rushes outside to play.

Page 20
1. Answers will vary but may include adjectives such as *mean, unkind, scary,* and *scared.* 2. Answers will vary but may include adjectives such as *kind, cooperative,* and *friendly.* 3–5. Answers will vary.

Page 21
1. B; 2. C; 3. F, T, T, F; 4. Answers will vary.

Page 22
1. Answers will vary but should include that the animals are scared at the beginning of the poem. The animals ran and the giraffes ran for cover. 2. The animals are relieved because Ella did not sneeze. 3. Answers will vary but should include the idea that couplets are pairs of lines that rhyme.

Pages 23–24
A–D. Answers will vary. E. Answers will vary but may include *hid* or *covered.* F–L. Answers will vary. M. (1) Dad plants the seeds in the garden. (2) Mom waters the seedlings. (3) Dad puts the flowers in a vase. (4) He gives the flowers to Mom for her birthday. N. tiny, turtle, took, turn; sassy, silly, snake; O–P. Answers will vary.

Answer Key

Page 25
1. B; 2. C; 3. Answers will vary but should include that *destroy* means to damage or ruin. 4. Answers will vary, but may include: Bees move pollen from one flower to the next. Bees produce honey. Ladybugs eat the bugs that chew our plants. Spiders catch flies, crickets, and moths in their webs.

Page 26
1. A; 2. Students should underline *It was a hard and long ride.* 3. Answers will vary but should include that many years ago, the Pony Express carried mail across the United States. 4. Answers will vary.

Page 33
1. C; 2. A; 3. Yes. Answers will vary but may include that Koko identified herself in the photo when Dr. Patterson asked her about it. 4–5. Answers will vary.

Page 34
1. Answers will vary but should include that *frightening* means scary or alarming. 2. Answers will vary but should include that *hasty* means sudden or rapid. 3. Answers will vary but may include: feeling rain on a hot day, feeling a gentle breeze on your skin, or getting to play in the snow. 4. Answers will vary but may include: too much rain can cause a flood, strong winds can cause a tornado, or you cannot always travel in a snowstorm.

Page 35
1. Answers will vary but may include: The Heart: The heart moves blood through your body. Both: You must exercise to keep your heart and lungs healthy. It is good to make your heart and lungs work harder sometimes. The heart and lungs are an important part of your body. The Lungs: Without lungs you could not breathe. 2. Answers will vary but should include that your heart will beat faster. 3. Answers will vary.

Page 36
1. A; 2. (1) It uncovers its lights by opening its eyelid. (2) It swims in a straight line. A dangerous fish follows the lights. (3) The flashlight fish covers its lights. (4) It turns and races away. 3. B; 4–5. Answers will vary.

Page 37
1. Answers will vary but may include phrases such as *consist of* or *are composed of*. Sentences will vary. 2. 1. C, 2. A, 3. B; 4. Answers will vary but may consist of examples such as people often help each other; you might walk your neighbor's dog; you might go to the store for your grandmother; or the neighbors may invite you to the movies.

Answer Key

Page 38

1. C; 2. Students should circle *What's on the Menu?* and *Home, Sweet Home.* 3. Answers will vary but may include that both paragraphs are about insects and give information about butterflies and bees. The first paragraph gives characteristics of insects. The second paragraph gives information about what insects eat.
4. Answers will vary, but possible answers include: Insects live in different kinds of homes. Supporting details may vary, but possible answers include: Bees build hives from wax; Ants and termites build hills on the ground; Some insects like mayflies and damselflies spend most of their lives underwater.

Page 39–40

A–E. Answers will vary. F. Students should cross out C. G–J. Answers will vary. K. Students should underline *Seeds move from one place to another.* L–P. Answers will vary.

Page 41

1. L, L, L, S, L; 2. S, S, L, L, S; 3. light, tie; 4. rain, stay; 5. clean, green; 6. boat, crow; 7. teep; 8. qay; 9. fow; 10. stight; 11. table; 12. music; 13. silent; 14. relax

Page 42

1. S, L, L, S, L; 2. L, S, S, S, L; 3. tight, pie; 4. wait, gray; 5. meal, queen; 6. coach, slow; 7. laim; 8. mie; 9. soam; 10. veat; 11. secret; 12. belong; 13. paper; 14. hotel

Page 53

October in the Orchard: 1. The apples are bright red, golden yellow, and green.
2. Answers will vary but should include words like *dripped, oozed,* and *leaked.* 3. Answers will vary but should include that the story could really happen because a family could really visit an apple orchard, pick apples, and take them home. 4. Answers will vary but should include that one of the children is telling the story. You can tell because the child talks about "Daddy."
A Group Game:1. The directions are for the game charades. 2. You need a pencil and some slips of paper. 3. You can write song titles, book titles, or movie titles. 4. Answers will vary.
A Fright in the Night:1. Answers will vary but should include that the story takes place in the past because Josh lit a candle and put a bar down over the door to close it. 2. Possible answers include: *little, dark, front, two, great, big,* or *furry.* 3–4. Answers will vary.
Go with the Snow!:1. Snowboarders need boots and snowboards. 2. surfing, skateboarding, and skiing; 3. Possible answers include: they can ride backward, spin, do a wheelie, or grab. 4. Answers will vary.

Page 54

A. beat, braid, vote, known, chief, sheep; B. frog, hand, hug, fell, gift, bend; C. 1. lake, 2. rain, 3. May, 4; brave; D. 1. beak, 2. tree, 3. seal, 4. sheep; E. 1. high, 2. die, 3. wide, 4. bright; F. 1. road, 2. snow, 3. joke, 4. home; G. 1. huge, 2. mule, 3. cube, 4. use; H. 1. broken, 2. spider, 3. beyond, 4. fable

Answer Key

Page 59

skool, frend, i, we, road, ., hert, callt, After school, my friend and I went to the park. We played soccer. We rode our bikes. My friend fell and hurt his leg. I called his mom for help. walkeng, ., wil, by, froot, movees, .; We are walking to the store. My sister will meet us there. She will buy some fruit for us. Then, we will go to the movies.

Page 60

1–10. Check students' work. Answers will vary.

Pages 61–62

A. the, the, ., hop; B. i, walk, ., stoped, he; C. i, that, hi, . , treez; D. ., blew, Blew, Win, don, .; E. my, it, i, sea, lynn, .; F. tooth, cricket; G. bike, dog; H. brush, vacuum; I. 1. apron, 2. bonus, 3. hotel, 4. began; J. 1. cradle, 2. alone, 3. sleepy, 4. lady; K. 1. spray (also prays); 2. faint; 3. snail (also slain or nails); 4. gray; L. 1. wheat; 2. knee (also keen); 3. seed; 4. clean; M. 1. might; 2. lie; 3. sight; 4. knight; N. 1. throw; 2. coast; 3. flown; 4. groan; O–P. Answers will vary.

Pages 63–64

1. dresses; 2. parks; 3. colony; 4. troop; 5. dice; 6. wives; 7. My brother's dog is in the house. 8. myself; 9. themselves; 10. herself; 11. talked; 12. goes; 13. came; 14. rose; 15. large, eight, hairy; 16. two, hot, cheesy; 17. quickly, carefully; 18. inside, easily; 19. Tracy and Fred walked to the zoo. 20. We baked cupcakes and cookies. 21. sue, hawaii; 22. nick, valentine's; day; 23. January 31, 2018; 24. I want to visit Houston, Texas. 25. My sister likes to skate, cook, and read. 26. I'm

Pages 65–66

1. boxes; 2. lights; 3. caravan; 4. forest; 5. men; 6. moose; 7. Where is my sister's doll? 8. himself; 9. yourselves; 10. ourselves; 11. pulled; 12. swam; 13. found; 14. put; 15. cold, icy, blue; 16. spicy, hot; 17. loudly, nearby; 18. often, always; 19. She washed the dishes and the clothes. 20. A fish and a turtle swam in the pond. 21. Mark, Christmas, november; 22. miller, city, zoo, tuesdays; 23. September 13, 2017; 24. My favorite colors are green, pink, and purple. 25. I live in Smithtown, Ohio. 26. She'll

Page 67

1. un/happy; 2. bi/cycle; 3. re/build; 4. pre/school; 5. to build again; 6. not happy; 7. worth/less; 8. grace/ful; 9. garden/er; 10. love/less; 11. full of grace; 12. a person who gardens; 13. flowerpot; 14. wheelchair; 15. B

Page 68

1. re/write; 2. pre/pay; 3. un/pack; 4. bi/weekly; 5. to pay before; 6. to write again; 7. teach/er; 8. price/less; 9. truth/ful; 10. hope/ful; 11. without price; 12. full of hope; 13. sandbox; 14. newspaper; 15. C

Page 71

1. parents; 2. classes; 3. teachers; 4. gifts; 5. posters; 6. clowns; 7. boxes; 8. books; 9. trips; 10. nights

Page 72

1. bouquet; 2. den; 3. hive; 4. litter; 5. pack; 6. deck; 7. clan; 8. flock; 9. school; 10. herd; 11–12. Answers will vary.

Answer Key

Page 73
1. oxen; 2. wolves; 3. sheep; 4. people;
5. wives; 6. feet; 7. deer; 8. loaves; 9. geese;
10. women; 11. halves; 12. children; 13. S;
14. P; 15. P; 16. S; 17. P; 18. S; 19. P; 20. S;
21. P

Page 74
1. itself; 2. myself; 3. themselves; 4. yourself;
5. ourselves; 6. himself; 7. yourselves;
8. herself; 9. ourselves; 10. himself; 11. itself;
12. myself

Page 75
New verbs will vary. Action verbs are:
1. walks; 2. dances; 3. play; 4. saw;
5. moved; 6. left; 7. jumped; 8. threw

Page 76
1. got; 2. drew; 3. hurt; 4. ate; 5. choose;
6. froze; 7. paid; 8. wore; 9. shut; 10. fell;
11. caught; 12. spoke

Page 77
Across: 1. striped; 4. hot; 5. silly; 6. one;
7. sleepy; Down: 1. smoothly; 2. daily;
3. below; 6. often

Page 78
1. AV; 2. A; 3. N; 4. A; 5. V; 6. N; 7. V;
8. AV; 9. N; 10. A; 11. V; 12. AV

Page 79
1. A; 2. C; 3. B; 4. B; 5. B; 6. A; 7. A; 8. C

Page 80
1. monday, memorial day; 2. may, eve,
mother's, day; 3. south, dakota, montana, june;
4. we, thanksgiving, thursday, november;
5. pete's, oceanside, campground, florida;
6. julie, independence, day, july

Page 81
June 3, 2018
Dear Olivia,
   Hello! I am writing to tell you about my trip.
Mom, Dad, and I went to see my grandmother.
She lives in Tampa, Florida. She used to live in
Omaha, Nebraska. She moved to Florida on
February 21, 2017. She was tired of the snow.
   On the way to Florida, we stopped in
Atlanta, Georgia. Mom wanted to visit my aunt,
uncle, and cousins. They had a big party for
us. My aunt served pizza, cake, and chips. We
had a lot of fun!
   My grandmother was so happy to see us!
She took us to the beach. We went swimming,
surfing, and sailing. I took pictures of shells,
dolphins, and the pier. I cannot wait to go
back!
   Write to me soon!
Your friend,
Kathy

Page 82
1. won't; 2. What's; 3. She's; 4. we're;
5. you'll; 6. I'm; 7. It's; 8. can't; 9. She'll;
10. I've

Page 83
1. Polly's bike is yellow. 2. Have you seen my
dad's car? 3. The clock's hands are not moving.
4. The dog's bone is under the tree.
5. Where is Keith's football? 6. My sister's
phone is broken. 7. My cousin's friend met us at
the store. 8. The skunk's tail is black and white.

Page 84
1. recover; 2. biweekly; 3. uncertain;
4. preview; 5. read before; 6. view again;
7. to undo the knots; 8. careless; 9. catcher;
10. joyful; 11. someone who gardens; 12. full
of grace; 13. without a cord

Answer Key

Page 85

1. earring; 2. beachball; 3. fishbowl;
4. sailboat; 5. lunchbox; 6. sandcastle;
7. nighttime; 8. rattlesnake; 9. gumball;
10. fireplace

Page 86

1. B; 2. A; 3. C; 4. B; 5. A; 6. B; 7. B; 8. A

Pages 87–90

A. 1. boxes, 2. girls, 3. gloves, 4. colors,
5. misses; B. 1. cars, 2. parks, 3. brushes,
4. messes, 5. keys; C. 1. lives, 2. selves,
3. wives, 4. scarves, 5. leaves; D. 1. deer,
2. mice, 3. women, 4. sheep, 5. feet;
E. 1. swarm, 2. bunch, 3. batch; F. 1. brood,
2. school, 3. pack; G. 1. ourselves, 2. itself,
3. themselves; H. 1. herself, 2. yourself,
3. myself; I. 1. floats, 2. walks, 3. stacks,
4. writes, 5. chases; J. 1–3. Answers will vary.
K. 1. dug, 2. hid, 3. knew, 4. won; L. 1. fell,
2. kept, 3. lost, 4. bit; M. 1. colorful, 2. one,
3. scary; 4. red; N. 1. carefully; 2. outside;
3. loudly, 4. tomorrow; O. Nouns: doll, cat;
Verbs; riding, sleeping; Adjectives: green, tall;
P. Nouns: monkey, theater; Verbs; moving,
climbing; Adjectives: quiet, little; Q. The green
balloon and the white balloon are in the air.
R. Tina wants turkey and cheese on her
sandwich. S. 1. iowa, sunday, 2. may, stan,
3. the, tuesdays, 4. my, rusty; T. 1. my,
december; 2. ann, new, york; 3. our, lake,
drive; 4. november, utah; U. Dear Frank, How
are you? I am well. I am writing from Houston,
Texas. I will be at your house soon! Love, Paul;
V. Dear Lisa, Will you come to my party? It is
on August 20, 2018. I hope to see you! Your
friend, Mary; W. 1. shouldn't, 2. she's,
3. we've, 4. they're, 5. didn't; X. 1. she'll,
2. they've, 3. it's, 4. couldn't; 5. we're;
Y. 1. my teacher's lunch, 2. my dog's bone,
3. the bug's wing; Z. 1. my brother's baseball,
2. the baby's rattle, 3. the clock's hands;
AA. 1. replay, 2. unable, 3. unhappy,
4. rewind; AB. 1. careful, 2. hopeless,
3. helpful, 4. worthless; AC. 1. doghouse,
2. mailbox, 3. notebook, 4. applesauce;
AD. 1. roadwork, 2. hairbrush, 3. fireplace,
4. bedroom; AE. 1. B, 2. C; AF. 1. A, 2. B